INVESTING FOR FUN—
AND PROFIT©

Investing for Fun— and Profit©

Frank Stovall

To order additional copies of this book, contact:
Xlibris Corporation
1-888-795-4274
www.Xlibris.com
Orders@Xlibris.com
55783

CONTENTS

I dedicate this book to my
wife, Marjorie,
who in my eyes has been the best friend,
wife, mother, and grandmother in the world.
Her constant support and contribution
to my every endeavor
has been more than any
ordinary individual should ever expect.
She is the love of my life.

Acknowledgements

I want to thank my good friend, Kathy DeWitt, for typing the first half of the manuscript. Reading my writing is no small accomplishment and without her this book would never have gone to press.

I also want to thank Sylvia Everett of Sylvia's Secretarial Services for completing the manuscript typing. Her "Professionalism with a personal touch" is an excellent motto and it describes her services to a "T."

FOREWORD

It is rare, maybe unprecedented, that one can view practically an entire financial life of another individual. Growing up in the Depression, the author knew the value of a dollar, even a dime, and developed a habit of keeping detailed financial records: a practice that he followed through senior adulthood. Herein is a summation of those records.

This is a book about investing—but not about getting rich. It is a book about one person's—a novice—experience in which he had a learning experience, fun and profit all at the same time. It is a well documented record of both land and stock investing over a period of more than fifty years. There were both losses and profits, but fortunately the profits came out ahead. The author is a gambler at heart, but never in his 87 years did he make a bet for money (other than land and stocks). Even with the current craze over lottery he has never bought a lottery ticket. But he had fun trying to get the right stocks, to buy at the right time and to sell at least not at the wrong time.

This book started as a documentation of stock investments. When I reached the point in time that I invested in land, I decided to include material written back in 1977. Later it seemed appropriate to include records of our investment in our children's education. From a tax savings standpoint it made sense to include appreciated stock charitable donations; thus the inclusion of our financial involvement in church activities. The need to assist our grown children in housing purchases brought in those records. Thus, this book evolved into a book on "life investments," not just investments.

As this manuscript goes to final type, the financial structure has just experienced the greatest stress since the Great Depression. In less than one week the Dow fell over ten percent. Crisis though it is to those who have lost jobs, the next six months may well offer the greatest buying opportunity for stocks in many, many years. The ride back up may be slow, but for quality stocks, it will be very productive.

CHAPTER I

Early Stock Investments

This book is not an investment primer, although a novice can probably learn from it. Whereas most financial books and articles are written by experts and savvy financial gurus, this book is simply a record kept by one non-financial individual. Chapters 2 through 8 were exactly as written in 1977. The remaining chapters were written in 2005-08.

The profits achieved over the fifty year period, except for the recent few years, are not great, but they were steady profits. The financial capability of the author is not out of the ordinary in the least—he cannot claim to be able to professionally read a financial statement. But over the years there were several basic principles:

1. Never invest money that I can't reasonably afford to lose.
2. Diversity
3. Invest in something
4. Don't be afraid to sell winners or losers.

Retirement planning is not getting any easier. With the shift from company sponsored retirement plans to 401-K, the individual is increasingly responsible for retirement investment decisions. What do you know about investments? In college my track coach said "You guys don't know the difference between stocks and bonds". For me, as an engineering student, he wasn't far wrong. A few years later I decided to learn. Recorded herein are records of my experience. Following my experience won't make you a fortune, but one can see first hand how a novice went about developing a rather successful investment program.

My first experience with stocks was in the early 50's while I was on Navy recall with three small children. Success was not overwhelming, but I ended the 50's with a profit. And I enjoyed selecting stocks that I thought were good investments. Then in the 70's with my financial position much better I took a chance on a land investment—with terrible results. The land investment is documented in considerable detail after a brief summary of early stock investments.

This book was started way back in the seventies. A Foreword, written in 1977, reflects situations that are strikingly similar to today's conditions.

1977 Foreword

With all the scandals that have rocked our nation in recent years (Watergate, Korean payoffs, congressional sex scandals, industrial bribes to foreign governments, price fixing, etc.) an in-depth examination of the financial affairs of a fairly typical, honest, law abiding American family may be of interest.

This book describes the financial affairs of a family that started with nothing and ended up with a modest estate. With a little more ability and luck they might have been well off financially. With a little less determination and financial management they could have ended up where they started: solvent but without reserves or retirement security.

In 1950 while on Navy recall at age 30 I decided I would be motivated to learn about business if I owned some stock, so I contacted a broker and bought a few shares of stock based upon his recommendation. Shortly thereafter, I purchased a few shares in a stock that was mentioned in a News periodical. Most of the early investments were losers, but one or two winners offset the losses. And so I was encouraged to continue investing.

At this time we had three children, a ten year old car, a house that was completed less than a year earlier, a loan for virtually the entire cost of the house, and net assets that couldn't have been more than $5,000. I did have a college degree and was a lieutenant in the Navy Reserve reluctantly recalled to active duty. My background was strictly non-financial. My father finished only the sixth grade and worked most of his life as a mechanic. I graduated in engineering and never took a course that dealt with stocks and bonds.

My broker suggested funds (actually only one because there were very few funds back then) and individual stocks. Since I wanted to be connected with individual companies I selected stocks. Investment in a fund would probably have been a wiser move, but I wanted to wheel and deal in stocks. Since my available money was quite restricted, I purchased in 1951 100 shares of Television Equipment Corporation at $0.25 per share followed a little later by purchasing 1000 shares at $0.10 per share for a total investment of $125.00. I then purchased a quantity of shares of Admiral Corporation.

The Television Equipment Corporation later went bankrupt (1953) and I sold the Admiral stock for a profit.

In 1952 I purchased:

Ultrasonics
Seapack Corporation
Missouri Research Corporation
Admiral Corporation
ConVair Aircraft

I lost money on the first three stocks and made money on the other two.

The stock broker recommended a new stock that made tape for the then new tape recorders. He also recommended stock in Teleprompter, new to the TV industry. I rejected both.

The next year I moved away from speculative stocks and became more familiar with recognizable companies. In TIME Magazine I read an article about the aircraft manufacturer Glen L. Martin. Further purchases and sales were:

American Bosch	$384.00 loss
Glen L. Martin Aircraft	$454.00 gain
Net Gain	70.00

The year 1954 showed more investment progress. There were four gains and two losses from previous year purchases. The year 1955 was significant in that I repurchased and sold at a profit American Bosch, a stock that was a loser in 1953. In 1956 I made more in dividends than I did in stock sales: $185.00 in dividends and $150 net profit from sales of Lockheed and Chrysler. The year 1957 was similar to 1956 in that there was $257 in dividends and a net loss of $550 in stock sales of J & L Steel, Owen Corning Fiberglass, Daystrom, and Lockheed. The chickens really came home to roost in 1958 and 1959. Earlier purchases were sold with a gain of only $700 and losses of $1,850. Good dividends eased the pain. The fifties ended with a slight gain.

Looking over the data for the sixties shows no remarkable investments, with a gain ($6,000) over the decade. Most of the gains were used as church donations, thus paying no tax on the appreciation. Today a gain of $6,000 seems like very little, but in almost 50 years we have had inflation somewhere between ten and twenty. A ten fold increase would make this gain equivalent to $60,000.

See Figures 1, 2, and 3 for more details of transactions in the 1950's and 60's.

In the seventies I seemed to have learned something from the 50's and 60's in that I churned (bought and sold) less and mainly made charitable donations with stock that had appreciated. For reasons unknown I have virtually no stock records for the seventies. For one thing, we had three in college (Rick, the oldest, graduated in 1969) with the last graduating in 1978. According to my Lockheed Savings Plan records, the period 1971-1975 was either flat or negative. The period 1976-1979 was much better.

What little records that I have indicated that I donated $7,500 in appreciated stock to our church in the seventies. More significant, in 1975 I invested and lost well over $30,000 in a land purchase in Henry County, Georgia.

Figure 1—Stock Transactions in the Fifties 1950-1959

	Gain*	Loss*
Television Equipment Corporation		1
Lockheed	1	1
Admiral TV	3	3
Zenith TV	1	1
Ultrasonics Corporation		1
Seapak Corporation (Seafood)		1
Missouri Research Corporation		1
Glidden Paint	2	
Texas Pacific Land Trust		1
Convair Aircraft	1	
American Bosch (Electronics)	2	1
Glen L. Martin Aircraft	1	
Muntz TV (Bankrupt)		1
Chrysler Auto	1	2
Giant Portland Cement	3	
Hertz	1	
Sylvania	1	
Montgomery Ward	1	3
Jones & Laugren Steel		1
Owens-Corning Fiberglass		1
Daystrom		1
Monsanto	1	
I T & T	1	
Cross Machinery		1
General Dynamics		2
Sperry Rand	1	
Ford	1	
Western A & B		1
G. M.	1	
Rich's Department Store	1	
Raytheon	1	

* times traded

Note: Net Gain $700 plus $1,000 dividends plus $400 gain to church

Figure 2—Stock Transactions in the Sixties 1960-1969

	Gain*	Loss*
John Deer Tractor	1	
Woolworth	1	
Lockheed	1	4
Hertz	1	
Canadian Marconi	2	
Giant Portland Cement	1	
Federal Pacific Electric	3	2
I T & T	4	
Clevite		1
FMC	1	
Spec. Elec. Development		2
Wilcox Gay		1
Armalite	1	
RCA	1	
Atlanta Gas Company	1	
Acoustica		2
Electronic Associates	1	
Admiral TV	1	
United Family Life		1
Harvey Aluminum	1	
Canadian Superior Oil	1	
Sperry Rand	1	
Revlon	1	

* times traded

Figure 3—Early Stock Investment Summary

Year	Types of Securities	Gain*	Loss
1952-53	Aircraft, Ford	450	
	Television, Auto Accessories/Defense		320
1954	Cement, Paint, Aircraft	1,800	
	Television		500
1955	Cement, Auto Accessories/Defense	935	
	Miscellaneous		150
1956	Aircraft, Auto	150	
1957	Steel, Fiberglass		300
	Aircraft		250
1958	Electronics, Automobiles		1,450
1959	Electronics, Department Store, Cement	700	
	Auto rental, Aircraft, department store		400
1960	Aircraft, Auto Rental	300	
1961	Electronics	350	
	Electrical		350
1962	Electrical, speculative stocks		1,150
1963	Aluminum Fabricators	600	
	Telephone	100	
1964	Electronics, telephone, gas	1,000	
1965	Electronics speculation		800
	Electrical	500	
1966	TV, Telephone, Computers	1,350	
1967	Electronics speculation		750
	Electrical	1,450	
1968	Aircraft, Electronics, Electrical	1,500	
	Insurance		100
1969	Oil, computers, cosmetics	2,350	
	Aircraft		550

* plus dividends and interest

CHAPTER II

The Big Land Investment—1977

Thirty thousand dollars. What could I do if I had thirty thousand tax free dollars? What would I do if I had it back! Many books have been written about those who made a million—or even hundreds of millions. For John Q. Public, however, a more familiar situation is to work and slave to save, invest, and maybe acquire a few extra bucks that can come in handy in the retirement years.

In my case, I lost over $30,000 in a bad land investment—or a good investment at a bad time. For millions of other people the figure might be $3,000 or $300,000. The principle is the same. After the fact we ask ourselves what we did wrong, what can we learn for the next try, should we have spent the money in the first place instead of being a little risky and trying to grow more money.

Again, I ask myself the question:

What could I do if I had it back? I could set my middle son up in business, or help my youngest son finish college and go through medical school. I could pay off the debts of our oldest son and our daughter, both heavily in debt from completing graduate work in medical school and law school, respectively. I could make a significant contribution toward an organ for our church. Or my wife and I could take vacations from the South Seas to Switzerland. Or I might stash it away and take early retirement, for at 8 percent interest it would produce $2,400 per year to supplement what retirement I will get from my company, together with what I'll eventually get from Social Security.

To some, this amount of money may seem like a fortune. To others it is but a pittance. But to me it is a half life-time of savings. I am far from destitute as a result of this loss, but it would be miles from the truth to imply that I suffer losses like this all the time. I have been working for a living for 35 years. In that time I have managed to pay for a house and acquire equity in other assets worth maybe a total of $60,000. On average, then, other than my house this loss represents more that half my lifetime savings.

If I had it to do over again, would I save this money or spend it? To answer this question, even to myself, requires some examination of my family background, my wife, my children, my concept of financial management, a little of my philosophy, my idiosyncrasies, and my capabilities and limitations.

Thirty thousand dollars! How did we ever save up that much money to lose? We had nothing left over after the bills were paid for so long that it seemed that we had no savings at all. It wasn't easy. Then twelve years ago we had our first exposure to college. With each of our kids working to pay part of their expenses and all of their spending money, we spent an average of $2,500 per year per child—$32,500 to date. Three years ago it looked as though we were over the hump—only one left in college after having three in college at one time, then only two, and now down to only one. We had become so accustomed to austere living that we could survive for one more year—invest in a land deal and pick up a few extra dollars—even extra thousands of dollars hopefully. All we needed was $20,000 down, pay interest on the $60,000 mortgage, and sell for a profit in about a year. We raised $8,000 from loans on our insurance, sold $6,000 in stocks that we had purchased over the years, cashed in all of our government bonds, and by a slim margin made up the balance from savings. At least we weren't up to our ears in mortgages. I'm sort of a gambler at heart, but before I've been too conservative to over extend my financial resources. We ended up with virtually no cash, but no real outstanding debts. Our only asset was our house. Our biggest liability was the interest payments on the insurance loans and the interest payments on the land mortgage.

Why did we take such a gamble? "Everybody was doing it, I guess. Many of our friends had made small fortunes over the previous three or four years. They would invest in property, pay interest for six or eight months, sell for a 25% increase, and quickly recover their investment plus an easy $20,000-$30,000. The prospects in this case looked like this:

Outlay:	$1,000 principal one year
	$4,000 interest one year
	$5,000
Possible Sale Income:	$32,000 over our purchase price
	- $ 5,000 outlay in principal and interest
	$27,000 net gain in less than a year

A twenty-seven thousand dollar profit in only one year. And all I had to do was to "loan" my $20,000 for one year and make the one $5,000 principal and interest payment. It looked too good to be true. But I knew that it had been true—I had followed several previous investments and they all made handsome profits. Nothing illegal, immoral or unethical. Not even risky, or so it seemed at that moment. Three years later, however, I see an entirely different picture:

3 year outlay:	$ 3,000 principal
	$12,000 interest
	$15,000

| 1977 potential sale price | $24,000 less than our purchase price |
| | $39,000 potential loss |

Anyway you look at it, this investment was sour. If we toss in the towel, we have lost $39,000. Since Uncle Sam takes from the successful it is only fair that he help out the unsuccessful. And he does, to a limited extent. Tax credits on interest and loss will bring the net deficit down by about $9,000 to a "mere" $30,000.

But the economy is picking up. In two years the property may be worth what we paid for it. Or, it may not be. If it is, we will have invested another $5,000 per year in order to salvage the $24,000 that we will lose on the purchase price. We will still have lost all our interest payments for the past years plus the next two years. In essence, the decision is to spend another $10,000 to save $14,000 ($24,000 - $10,000). And it is not a sure thing. The economy could get worse instead of better. Decision: Toss in the towel.

Imagine being thankful that you're "only" going to lose $30,000. That is exactly our situation as this is being written. When we negotiated this contract, I was so sure that I would never default on it that I signed all the papers instead of having my wife do so. Since our house and most of our material possessions are in my name, if there should be any flaw in the foreclosure for our abandonment of this property, then I would stand to lose other property in partial payment for the land. Had my wife purchased the land there would have been relatively little additional risk since she owns no other property (no longer true in 2006).

The question of disagreement between partners has never come up in this situation. But think of the possibilities! Here we are, six parties brought together by a mutual friend. Three of us are close friends, and the other three were total strangers to us. Because of the mutual friendship, we assumed that everything would go all right. And it has been. Of the six, only one wanted to continue to make payments rather than to abandon, but suppose only one had wanted to abandon. How would we have resolved the problem of his payments? None of us was prepared to take on still more obligation. We could barely carry what we had. Such are the potential problems of joint ownership.

CHAPTER III

Investments and Our Family—1977

It has long been my economic philosophy that for one to live very far above average, assuming no family fortune to count on, would require wise investments. In my opinion, ordinary income from a salary just won't hack it. Of course there is always the exception, the doctor, the smart lawyer, the president of a large corporation, etc. I still hold that opinion, though it is obviously shaded by my own experience of a not-so-wise investment and my look back at where I would be without the investment. I took the big plunge and lost. But suppose I had made the same investment two or three years earlier. I'd probably have an additional $20,000-$100,000 to retire on.

On the other hand, suppose I had spent that $30,000 over the last ten years, which is about the period that I earned it. What would I have done with it? I'd probably invest it again but hopefully with better timing, trying to build up something for retirement. But suppose I had decided to spend at a higher rate. What impact would it have had on my and my family?

Ten years ago my oldest son was a junior in college. Because of the cost he did not come home from college in Massachusetts from September until Christmas. During two school years we could have flown him home six times for weekends/holidays for a total cost of about $1,000. To meet expenses, he worked part time. He could have had more campus freedom if we had contributed the $1,500 that he earned at his job.

Ten years ago our daughter was a freshman in college. To my knowledge she never really needed anything that she didn't have, but she certainly never had the best of many things. An automobile on the campus was a common thing, but she didn't really need a car. School was only seven hours away by car, but it wrecked a weekend. A few more trips home by airplane might have been worthwhile, but certainly not a necessity. A $1,000 sprinkled here and there might have been very helpful, but we really didn't know where it was needed. She also worked part time during part of her college, and an extra contribution of $1,500 to her education would have made things easier, though not necessarily better.

Our middle son was in the tenth grade ten years ago. Money was never one of his needs. He worked hard, made more than he spent and that practice continued on through college. If we had spent a couple thousand dollars extra along the way would it have made him different and better? Different, certainly yes. Better? Possibly. But possibly not as good. Who knows?

Our youngest son was in the sixth grade ten years ago. Since he is the youngest and our income has increased with time, he has had a little more of everything (except college expense allowance) than the others. As far as I can see he has neither profited nor suffered from more abundance, not that it was a whole lot more. He is now a senior in college, and he is trying to save a few dollars for graduate school. Since he was the last of the clan, he has had full use of the old car since he became a sophomore. To gain freedom in its use he purchased it from us about a year ago.

Ten years ago, my wife and I had been married 23 years. We had a mortgaged house, a two year old Falcon automobile and a one year old Ford station wagon. Today our youngest son owns the Falcon; I drive the station wagon and my wife drives a 1965 Pontiac. In these ten years there have been a number of things that those in our economic circle have done that we have not done. For example, on our 25th wedding anniversary we discussed a trip to Hawaii, but we settled for a trip to the beach. A new car has not been on our agenda, since the old ones are good transportation. Expensive clothes have never been in our annual budget so there was no strong incentive for change.

Let's forget the past and try to look forward. Our youngest has only one more year of college. In the next couple of years we should be able to save a good bit of money unless we:

a. Give it to the kids
b. Have an unforeseen illness
c. Invest it unwisely
d. Suddenly lose my job or take early retirement

What should we do with the $10,000 that I hope to save in the years before I retire? We can save it for retirement but there is no present indication that we are going to be too strapped for money when we retire. We can help all four of our kids, but it appears that they can make it on their own, possibly except for some loans as down payment on houses. We can travel, except that time is at a premium now and won't be after retirement. We can get another car, and that could become a necessity since we now have over 125,000 miles on each of our cars. We can probably blow it in a thousand different ways, but it is difficult to identify what ways. Once the floodgate is opened to spending, all of a sudden there is not enough money to go around.

CHAPTER IV

Observations In 1977

In reflecting upon the loss of a large amount of money and evaluating what I might have done differently if I had a second chance, I arrive at some rather interesting observations. First, our first 20 years of marriage were, by necessity, rather austere. We started out with absolutely nothing save a diamond ring and an education. After ten years of marriage, we had served a world war, tripled the size of our family, paid a debt to Uncle Sam in a military recall for 18 months, and built a house. We lived within our income, but rarely had extra cash after the bills were paid and the bare necessities of life were met.

At the end of a second ten years we owned two almost new cars, had a house almost paid for, but still had very little left over for luxuries, with four growing children and 16 years of college ahead of us.

It was really not until after 30 years that we began to see more money coming in than was going out. My salary was higher, two of the kids were through college, the house was paid for, and all of a sudden there was a chance to relax from an economic standpoint. Then this land deal presents itself. It looked like the grand opportunity to finally have something. What I didn't realize at the time was that the real opportunity was to invest in 8% or 9% bonds, an investment which involved practically no risk.

Examination of things gone by reveal an almost miserly existence by some people's standards, but a rather adequate existence by the standards of most. I didn't say miserable, because it wasn't. But there was rarely money available for unnecessary events or pleasures. Suppose I had borrowed money (or repaid more slowly) on the house during the 20-30 year period. We could have lived a lot fancier. But would it have been better? I doubt it. I find that I have grown reasonably accustomed to austere living. Maybe I would be happier with more to spend, but probably not.

What about the last three years. It was that period that I had extra income, but it was all taken away in the great investment. The net result, of course, is that the last three years have been virtually a carbon copy of the previous thirty. What about the next three years, or the next thirty (and there may well be 30 more. I am 56 and 30 years from now, I'll be younger than the present age of my father.) The next 3 years should be good income years. If I take early retirement at 59, as I now consider a strong possibility, then the next 27 years may be austere again. I had better carefully examine the pros and cons on the retirement subject.

CHAPTER V

College & Higher Education Finances—1977

The question of parental responsibilities in college financial support is extremely complex. When our oldest child started to college, we endeavored to plan ahead so that there would be enough support but not too much. It was our plan to adequately provide college for all of our children without unduly penalizing our future or that of the remaining children.

In 1965 I was earning $18,000 per year, which appeared to be enough to adequately finance four kids through four years of college. We sat down and estimated the cost of living on campus at a state school and concluded that $2,500 per year was adequate, particularly when supplemented by summer jobs and other on-campus income. For us, however, it turned out to be fourteen years of private schools and two of state schools instead of all state schools. We stuck to our $2,500 per year, and the kids made up the difference with jobs and "non-financial need" scholarships. In looking back, I think it was a mistake to go to private schools. But discussion with all four of the kids indicates that they think otherwise; they are glad that they got to choose schools even though it was a financial burden for them most of the way.

Rick's undergraduate expenses looked like this:

	Tuition	Other	Total Expenses	College	Comments
1965	$1,200	$1,410	$2,610	Emory	$1,000 scholarship
1966	$1,395	$1,190	$2,585	Emory	$ 200 scholarship
1967	$1,950	$1,945	$3,895	Williams	
1968	$2,190	$2,505	$4,695	Williams	$ 850 scholarship
		$7,050	$13,785		

Lois's expenses were:

1968	$1,100	$1,435	$2,535	Wake Forest	$ 200 scholarship
1969	$1,250	$1,570	$2,820	Wake Forest	
1970	$1,650	$1,275	$2,925	Wake Forest	
1972	$1,700	$1,885	$3,585	Wake Forest	
		$6,165	$11,865		

Phil's expenses were:

1970	$1,400	$1,495	$2,895	Furman	
1971	$1,600	$1,265	$2,865	Furman	
1972	$1,050	$1,620	$2,670	Furman	
1973	$ 525	$1,875	$2,400	Univ. of GA	
1974	$ 540	$2,005	$2,545	Univ. of GA	
		$8,260	$13,375		

Ray's expenses were:

	Tuition	Other	Total Expenses	College	Comments
1974	$2,200	$1,570	$ 3,770	Wake Forest	$1,000 scholarship
1975	$2,400	$1,745	$ 4,145	Wake Forest	$1,000 scholarship
1976	$2,500	$2,000	$ 4,500 est.	Wake Forest	$1,000 scholarship
1977	$2,600	$2,400	$ 5,000 est.	Wake Forest	$1,000 scholarship
		$7,715	$17,415		

The so called Parkinson's Law states that expenditures will rise to meet income. This law is evident with college expenses. Each of our children worked summers and part time at least one year out of the four. Rick needed a car for his summer job after his junior year, so we purchased a $600 used car with plans to sell it at the end of the summer. Fall came and Rick was persuasive, so he ended up taking the car back to school. At graduation it became his principal graduation gift from us. A $600 used car was also purchased for Lois as a graduation gift, but she had use of the family old third car during part of her senior year. Phil bought his own car his sophomore year. He purchased a used sailboat with his $600 graduation gift. In keeping with our theory that students are better off without cars at school, Ray had no car the first year. However, we purchased our old third family car for $250 and, therefore, had wheels from his sophomore year on. It now has 125,000 miles and hopefully will not give up the ghost before graduation in 1978.

The money that goes into education! Rick has had eight years of post-graduate work, all on his (and his wife's) earnings and loans. He is now a doctor. Lois had three years post-graduate work, mostly on borrowed money and is now a lawyer. Phil aspires to be a real estate broker and has no inclination toward post-graduate education, and Ray's future education is yet to come. No part of the graduate effort has been family supported. Right or wrong, that's the way it has been. If necessary they can work a year or two before continuing their education. I and many others like me have done so, and it is not all bad.

There is no magic formula as to how much financial support parents should give their children during college. In our own case, we obligated 15% of our income the first year of our first child's college. It peaked at 20% during the five years that we had two in college at one time, and decreased to less than 10% during the 13th year of financial support. They could have used more support, but they apparently did not really need any more.

CHAPTER VI

Loss Lessons—1977

What have I learned from all of this? Maybe nothing, but I surely do have a number of strong feelings.

1. At the right time, there is a lot of money to be made in land.
2. Beyond the right time, there is a long, long dry spell in land. It produces no income of itself. It just consumes interest and taxes and legal fees and frustration.
3. Invest in land only when nobody else wants it.
4. One failure should not stop one from saving for the future, but it gives reason to reexamine the ratio of today's spending to savings.
5. I will never have a whole lot of extra money. I just had the most that I may ever have and I did not even realize it. But I am reasonably well off and expect to continue to be.
6. Over the earlier years, I bought and sold a great many stocks for investment and speculation. Land was new to me. I can see that there are many similarities, but also many differences. With a stock you can almost always sell it for something, even though greatly depressed. Most stocks earn some dividends for you, whereas land is a long-term investment with the spoils only to those who are able to pick the right time to buy and sell.

One principle that is very similar for land and stocks is to be very hesitant about buying when things are going great. The ideal for stocks would be to save money during the 3 or 4 year cycle that stocks are high, then to buy in several increments when stocks are low (as guided by the DJI) then sell at least 2 years after buying. For land it appears to me that almost any time in the last 20 years, would have been all right to buy except the period just preceding the deep recession that we just experienced. A key factor seems to be a low down-payment with an exculpatory clause in order to take your licks and run if the going gets too rough.

Transaction costs with stocks generally run about 1-2% to buy and the same to sell. With land the figure runs 10 each way by the time surveys, title search, etc. are involved (plus taxes).

Looking back I can see that I regularly get attracted to stocks when times are good. Then when stocks recede I never feel that I have enough cash reserve to invest further. Then when the market picks up, I have a tendency to want to invest again. I must discipline myself to buy when nobody wants stocks and sell when the market is up.

Chapter VII

My Future—1977—on

This loss and the writing of this material have encouraged me to take stock of my overall financial condition. I am within nine years of required retirement with my company. I am now eligible for early retirement, and I reach what is known as "85 points" in two years. This is a point beyond which retirement benefits increase very slowly as compared with previous years. Should I retire now while my health is good and I can enjoy the free time or do I continue to work at a job that I know, with a good income? Can I afford early retirement? How about two years from now? Should I make some changes in my insurance policies, such as convert all ordinary life policies to paid up insurance and take out a new term policy to cover the period from now until I begin receiving Social Security benefits? Should I convert my stocks into secure, high interest bonds in order to have more security? Should I sell what little land I own and convert the money into bonds, or would the tax on the profit from this investment be so great that I would be better off to wait until I retire and my tax rate is less.

All of the foregoing need to be examined and decisions made that are in keeping with our best future interests.

As an aide to my future decisions, I have made a "best estimate" of my assets 1944 until the present. This tabulation is shown in Appendix 1.

Chapter VIII

Monetary Decision Making—1977

Since I cannot read the minds of others, and I have conducted no survey to learn how other people manage their family incomes, I do not know how many people there are that function as I do. From my childhood until quite recently, virtually no decision was made without at least a casual consideration of the monetary impact. To some, this must seem like a heavy burden. To me, it is quite easy. I obviously make mistakes at times, and let the cost unduly influence a "pleasure" decision. But the decision itself is quite painless. If I want a new tennis racquet I simply weigh my need and desire versus the money availability and desired pleasure and make a decision. Some people apparently just buy on impulse if they have the money or the credit. Not I. I do not think that style living would be very comfortable for me if I had to live without monetary reserves. I saved money as a child, as a teenager, and in my early adult years. I spent money freely on those things that I wanted most, and did without other things. Just recently we purchased a used 1974 automobile. Naturally I would prefer a new car, but I just cannot justify in my own mind the extra $4,000 that a 1977 car would cost as compared with the $2,000 that I paid for a good used one. There are only a few blemishes on this car, but I could have them removed and obtain an as-new paint job for $300. I cannot justify that either, even though I would still be $3,700 ahead of the game as compared with a new car.

As I look back I can see many instances where my decisions were in error. I believe, however, that they were more right than wrong. As my financial obligations have become relaxed, I have judged that time and pleasure are worth more to me and savings are less necessary. As an example, ten years ago we rarely ate away from home. Now the cafeteria and the quick order place do not even count toward our eating out. We feel that we have been out on the town only when we eat at a luxury motel or dining room. Of course, our decreasing family size has exerted a strong influence on our ability to eat out. The cost used to be simply prohibitive with a family of six.

CHAPTER IX

Later Thoughts—2006

It has been almost 30 years since the big land deal. Since that time, the stock market has been on a steady rise, with periodic drops. Land prices have also gone up by several multiples.

Did I learn anything? Yes. I have invested in stocks and bonds, I have diversified, and I have sold half of individual stocks when a sustained price increase was in question. In retrospect, I should have sold more stocks closer to the peak but at least for many, I didn't sell too soon. Charitable donations were always made with appreciated stocks, thus paying no capital gains tax. I did not over-invest in any stock, but I came close to it with one that I could not imagine going way down: Lucent. The jury is still out on a bond that I could not believe would go bust: Delta Air Lines. At least Delta was paying 9¾% interest, far above the going rate, for over ten years. Another big loser was K-Mart (actually K-Mart was an earlier gainer). To offset the losses were several significant gainers: GE, Gulf Oil, BellSouth, Exxon-Mobil, Home Depot, Regions Financial and Merck.

As previously mentioned, for me, investing has been an educational endeavor turned hobby.

I have surveyed old income tax returns and the 1950-59 results, shown earlier in Figures 1 and 3, are summarized below:

    33 stocks traded
    Net gain $700
    Dividends $1,000
    Largest gain—Giant Portland Cement $1,525
    Largest loss—Chrysler $1,194

From 1960-69, I stayed closer to known stocks, but I was still in and out of the market. There was very little movement in the market but there were enough gains so that most of our church contributions were made with appreciated stocks, thus no tax on appreciation. Results were shown in Figures 2 and 3 and are summarized below:

> 23 stocks traded
> Net gain $6,000
> Dividends No record kept
> Largest gain—Federal Pacific Electric $2,610
> Largest loss—Acoustica $1,588
> Largest single investment—Lockheed $2,800, break even
> Gains on stocks to the church $7,600

In the 1970's there was a stock net gain of approximately $3,500 with losses from Lockheed and Teledyne and gains from Federal Pacific Electric and UV Industries. A gain of almost $39,000 was realized in the 1980's with significant gains from Gulf Oil and heavy losses from Po Folks, which went bankrupt. For the seventies through half of the nineties, no record was kept of gains for contributions to our church, but they were selected for appreciation. A listing is shown on Figure 4.

I retired at 62 in 1984 at a time when inflation was high and stocks were moderately priced. Proceeds from my Lockheed savings plan were evenly distributed to bonds (interest 13%) and stocks. These investments set the stage for an unbelievable stock appreciation in the 90's. As the bonds came due they were converted to stocks.

Anyone who had money could have made paper profits in the 90's. Most every stock I owned showed significant appreciation. With four children and seven grandchildren, we transferred a significant amount of stock to each of the children. It was then their decision to sell and pay tax on the gains or to retain. Some sold, some followed the roller coaster up and back down again. These stocks are listed in Figure 5. Net gains on stocks in the 90's that either I sold or transferred to church or to the children was over $100,000.

Details on stocks sold in the 80's and 90's are shown on Figure 6.

The year 2000 was a terrible year for stocks, particularly Lucent, which had paper losses approaching $30,000. Fortunately, in 1999 I decided not to be too greedy and sold one-half of several of the stocks that had gone way up. I expect to sell the remaining Lucent stock this year (2006) to partially offset gains on other stocks which were purchased prior to 2000.

Figure 4—Appreciated Stock to Our Church 1960-99

		Gross	Appreciation
1960	Hertz	855	248
1961	IT & T	950	350
1963	Armalite	1,120	607
		371	127
1964	RCA	1,091	547
	I T & T	488	200
	Atl. Gas	506	133
1965	Fed. Pacific Electric	1,227	501
	I T & T	384	284
1966	Electronic Assoc.	1,220	587
1967	Fed. Pacific Electric	2,200	1,460
1968	Fed. Pacific Electric	2,800	1,150
1969	Canadian Superior Oil	1,800	1,440
1972		2,000	
1973		868	
1974	Fed. Pacific Electric & UV Ind.	1,878	
1975	92 shares Gulf Oil	Unknown	
1979	100 Dana	2,750	
1983	30 IBM	2,936	
1984		3,300	
1985	Coca Cola	3,050	
1986	Integraph	3,500	
1988	Ford	2,650	
	Singer	7,382	
1990	40 Atl. Gas	1,220	
	20 AT&T	820	
1991	300 Symbol Tech	4,425	
	82 Dana	3,321	
1992	80 AT&T	2,210	
1993	183 BellSouth	10,362	
1994	199 Southern Bell	5,500	
	24 EDS	876	
1995	180 Wachovia	6,122	2,520
1996	135 Amoco	8,369	5,595
1997	100 Merck	9,150	6,000
1998	400 K-Mart	6,450	4,005
	10 Raytheon	534	Nil
1999	100 Johnson & Johnson	9,375	2,021
	100 Texas Instruments	9,338	6,900

Figure 5—Stock to Children 1995-2000

		Value at Gift Time	Cost	Appreciation at Time of Gift
Rick	400 Amgen	28,100	2,700	25,400
	260 Amgen	14,000	2,700	11,300
Lois	300 ST Micro	19,200	6,900	21,300
	100 ST Micro	9,000		
Ray	200 Adobe	26,000	4,300	21,700
	300 Adobe	11,400	10,031	1,369
Phil	1/3 Vacation House			
				81,069

Figure 6—Capital Gains/Loss—1980-1999

Year	Stock-Bond-Investment	Gain	Loss
1980		0	0
1981		0	0
1982	Bonds – Teledyne, Singer, Lear Seigler		3,798
1983	Giant Portland Cement	855	
	Sears	3,543	
1984	Gulf Oil	18,275	
	Sullair, A & P		1,700
1985	GM	491	
1986	Po Folks		3,909
	Int. Harvestor		1,123
	GM, IBM, C. Cola, Ga. Fed., Lotus, H. Depot, Sears	24,504	
1987	C. Cola, AVCO, Tri Con Fund	3,600	
	Po Folks		4,051
1988	Singer, Kraft	9,370	
	Po Folks		5,099
1989	Chronar		2,366
1990	Chronar		572
1991	Tri Con, T-Bond	1,234	
1992	T-Notes, Ga. Power Preferred Stock	6,024	
1993	T-Notes, Mun. Bonds	3,018	
	Sears	4,321	
	Navistar		2,868
1994	Symbol, Syntex, Bond, T. Note		3,754
	Muni Bond	1,122	
1995	MCI, T-Note, Health Image, Mesa		2,799
1996	Muni Bond, T. Note, Teledyne	1,549	
	Davis Waste, Nova, WMX		275
1997	Payless Cashway		6,262
	Merck, Atlantic SE Airways	8,656	
1998	Damark, Western Digital, LTV, Tel Mex		2,686
	Merck, G.P., Sou. Co., Unocal, Ford, H. Depot	22,939	
1999	Miller, Skyline Fund, Air Touch, Fulton Cty. Bond.		16,123
	Amgen, Texas Instr., Genentech, LSI Log., Motorola, Tel Mex, Oracle, T. Note	56,847	

CHAPTER X

Fund and Bond Investments

Following my plan to diversify, I invested small amounts over the years in several different funds. Since I have not kept good records of capital gains and dividends for funds, it is difficult to make a comparison with my stock investments. With only one exception, all of my fund investments produced gains, but I am unable to make any kind of comparison. I invested with Fidelity, T. Rowe Price, Skyline, Capello Rushmore and Tri-Continental.

In general, my bond investments were only fair except for immediately after my retirement in 1984 when interest rates were sky high. Later bond investments were mostly for diversification. Since 2000, I have bought mostly U.S. Government T-Notes with profits and proceeds from earlier bonds. I am now in a conservative mode. I purchase these securities through Treasury Direct, which can be reached by calling 1-800-722-2678 or via internet *www.treasurydirect.gov*.

My big beef with earlier bond buys was that through a broker the transaction fees were excessive. Bond funds through Vanguard have been very good. As previously mentioned, my big bond problem was a Delta bond purchased in 1993. Since it has paid a 9¾% interest it has not been a bad investment but the bond is now worth only 35% of the purchase price.

Chapter XI

Housing Investments

A friend of mine made a small fortune buying old houses, fixing them up (and sometimes renting them), and then selling for a profit. In my case, I built my own house in 1950, doing my own contracting, and have lived in it ever since. Total cost was around $25,000. Current tax valuation is slightly above $300,000. In 56 years it has appreciated by a factor of 12. My stock investments can't beat that. Of course there has been extended inflation, taxes, routine upkeep, and some major improvements. The house has also been in a growing location in a growing city.

When, in 1982, our youngest child and his wife purchased their second house, we offered to loan them the down payment with the lowest interest rate allowed by law. They preferred a joint venture similar to one we had when they purchased the first house, which was sold at a profit. The house cost $52,278 and sold four years later for $69,000, in round numbers a net gain of $16,700, which we shared according to a predetermined formula. As above, real estate was a good investment. On the surface this appears to be a profit of around 30%. In reality, it is much more than that because the down payment ($25,366) was much less than the purchase price. The sharing agreement is documented in Figure 7.

Figure 7—Agreement—1095 Creekdale Drive, Clarkston, GA 30021 dated 7/11/82

1. The total cost of above residence is $52,278.00, which includes $278.00 closing cost.
2. In consideration of $15,500.00 investment portion by F.A. and M.H. Stovall and $9,865.56 investment portion by R.L. and J.W. Stovall, profit or loss will be shared in the following ratio upon selling the house:

$$\text{FAS/MHS:} \quad \frac{15.5}{15.5 + 9.866} = \frac{15.5}{25.366} = 0.611$$

$$\text{RLS/JWS:} \quad \frac{9.866}{25.366} = 0.389$$

3. FAS and MHS will pay no upkeep, taxes, or further improvements.
4. Upon selling the residence, FAS and MHS will share in gain or loss in the ratio of 0.611. The gain or loss will be calculated by subtracting $52,278 from the net sales price (after deducting sales commission, etc. from sales price). If less than $25,366 cash is realized from the sale, FAS and MHS will receive 0.611 of the cash.
5. If the house is not sold when RLS/JWS leave the house, FAS and MHS will receive in cash, an amount to cover original investment and 0.611 profit based upon the average of two appraisals.

Sales Price	$52,000.00
Attorney Fee (W. Shows)	200.00
Loan Company Transfer Fee	45.00
Recording Deed to Secure Debt	3.00
Intan. Tax on Loan Deed	30.00
	$52,278.00

Other Closing Information

Earnest Money—Paid by FAS & MHS	$ 500.00
Additional Cash Investment by FAS & MHS	15,000.00
	$15,500.00

Cash Investment by RLS & JWS

$52,278 - (15,500 + 16,912.44 [loan] + 10,000 [2nd mortg.]) = $9,865.56
42,412.44

CHAPTER XII

Timing

What could be more important than timing? It's very important. I have already mentioned my very bad timing with real estate. In the late twenties my father saw the rapid rise of Coca-Cola stock and purchased stock in a drink call Nu-Grape. The 1929 crash took care of that investment and my father bought no more stock until he retired in 1950. During World War II, he purchased War Bonds, which he cashed in when he retired. He used the money to build a spec house, doing all the carpentry work himself. When he couldn't sell the house immediately, he panicked and sold for the out-of-pocket cost only. He called Merrill Lynch and obtained stock recommendations from a broker there. The recommendations were good and the timing was excellent, for the market was on a multi-year rise. His gains were significant.

One thing is for certain: no one can predict stock timing for sure. But one can recognize two things: the general market trend for years and years has been up, and there are cycles in market prices.

I was not smart enough in the late 1990's to predict the rapid rise in stock prices but I guess I was smart enough to sell about half of most internet stocks before the bubble burst. Yes, timing is important in buying and selling.

Another housing investment took place in 1987 when the lake house next to ours was on the market. Two of our sons and I purchased it for $130,000 with the idea of renting it during the summer months, with maintenance, etc. on a shared basis. Rental income barely covered maintenance, taxes, utilities, and insurance, but we did benefit from depreciation on our income taxes until the partnership was dissolved in accordance with a partnership agreement in 1998, at which time the valuation was $200,000. Today, the value is close to $300,000. A copy of the partnership agreement may be obtained free of charge as long as copies are available by sending $3.00 (for postage) to FPR, P.O. Box 332, Morganton, GA 30560.

Just today I was watching a "Charlie Rose" program on public television. He was interviewing Jeff Immelt, the CEO of General Electric. I concluded from the conversation that now may be the time to reinvest in General Electric stock. Half of their business is world-wide with much of it in India and China, both of which are growing rapidly. In 1993 I purchased GE stock for $3.86 per share and it is now worth $33 per share. Since I have sold three-fourths of my holdings at prices above the present price, it seems prudent to reinvest.

Chapter XIII

Investment Sources and Strategy

Although the sources for investment information are almost limitless, a good source for me for many years was Forbes magazine. I subscribed to Forbes for at least 30 years and am not sure why I finally decided not to continue. In addition to excellent articles about various companies, there were several analysts who were brave enough to recommend stocks which were likely to do better than the average. Many of my purchases were based upon their opinions. I also subscribed to Fortune magazine until it started publishing twice as often as it had previously, and I didn't have time to read it.

More recently, I have benefited from Money magazine and Business Week. For many years I was interested in the future of bio-tech stocks, but didn't see evidence of early profitability. Then in one of the Money magazines, I read about five of these companies and I elected to purchase two: Amgen and Genentech. Both served me extremely well. One of our sons is still the beneficiary of my early Amgen purchase.

A local weekly public TV program on Georgia businesses has been the source of several very profitable purchases. The owners/managers were interviewed and they appeared to be good, savvy people. One of my shortcomings might be that I don't purchase enough of each stock that I believe will succeed, but it is also a safeguard. In this regard, I slipped up with Lucent; I just didn't believe it would ever falter.

One of the well known, successful investors used to say, "get to know the management." Good advice, but for a novice this is very difficult, but the aforementioned local TV program did offer this opportunity.

Another well known, very successful investor advocates careful selection and holding stocks. This is probably extremely good advice, but not nearly as much fun. A review of Figure 1 does not reveal but one stock that I purchased in 1950-59 that would have been wise to retain for a long period of time. Bad selection on my part? A review of Figure 2 does not reveal anything better. In 1986 I sold Home Depot when it tripled in price. Would that I had held on to it. But I did repurchase later.

I believe that reinvesting dividends is a good idea, but I have shied away from it because I never know what my cost basis is. Two of my investments in which I did reinvest dividends have done extremely well: SBC Corporation which used to be Southwest Bell and Tri-Continental Corporation Fund. Each is probably worth twenty times the original investment, but of course I have reinvested the dividends. I have no idea what my cost basis is in either. A third investment is a tax free bond fund with reinvested dividends, which after ten years is worth barely more than I paid for it. This fund was recommended to me by a stock broker; but over the years I had many other good stock broker recommendations.

Investment opportunities can come from many directions. In the late 90's, Georgia deregulated natural gas. It seemed to me that the basic provider, Atlanta Gas and Light, would greatly benefit under deregulation, so I purchased a substantial amount of stock in AGL. In the five years since 1999, it has doubled in value and currently pays about 7% in dividends on the original investment.

Chapter XIV

The 2000's

How have I done since 1999? Not too bad at all, but the profits have been mostly from stocks that I purchased prior to 2000. The proceeds have mostly gone into CD's and Treasury notes with 5 year coupons. I anticipated an increase in interest rates and that took place. Because of our age, we will now invest very conservatively: mostly in bonds. Our current brokerage portfolios, which are equally divided between us, have net gains of approximately 18%.

As previously mentioned, the late nineties presented some excellent buying opportunities and Merck, Home Depot, Oracle, and Amgen each increased by over 300% in just three or four years. Likewise, Texas Instruments, LSI Industries, and Motorola increased over 200% in the same period. Each of these stocks were sold in the nineties before the big stock decline.

Earlier chapters showed gains and losses in the year sold, without reference to the length of time that the stock was held. An examination of stocks held for various lengths of time might be interesting. For the years 2000-2007 stocks sold are organized by years held and are shown in Figure 8. Examination of Figure 8 identifies well-known stocks that were excellent investments: General Electric, Exxon Mobil, and Genentech. Each of these stocks are worth more today than when they were sold. Maybe I sold too soon. By contrast, Lucent, K-Mart (original stock) and Delta Air Lines Bond are today worth less than when they were sold. I was fortunate to have sold when I did.

Diversification and Stock Selection

Over the years one of my principal guidelines has been to diversify and not over-invest in any stock. I obviously did not follow my self-imposed rule. That I lost over $39,000 on Lucent stock means that I invested even more. I was just too convinced that it was solid and I continued to purchase stock as it was declining. Back in the eighties I had a similar experience with Po Folks and Chronar, but the amount invested in each was significantly less than with Lucent. The Lucent experience was a repeat of "The Big Land Investment of 1977."

Reviewing data over the fifty year period shows that I picked roughly two stocks that appreciated for each one that declined. In addition, except for Lucent and one or two other stocks, I invested more in each stock that went up as compared with those that lost money. I would like to think that this success was skill and not all luck. Over recent years my primary investments were in well-known stocks and these panned out to eventually be the best income producers. Along the way, however, I endeavored to identify and make modest investments in stocks that I thought had the potential to have phenomenal growth. Early there was Ultrasonics, Seapak, Texas Pacific Land Trust, Lotus, Chronar, Symbol, Payless Cashway, and a few others that were very disappointing. More recently there was Hitachi, Equity Office Properties, Earthlink, Miller Industries, Cerus, Repros Therapeutics, Sharp, Xilinx, Cheniere Energy, and Valentis with about the same disappointing results. Recent modest investments in Conoco Phillips (up 50%), Devon Energy (up 200%), Duke Energy (up 30%), Kyphon (up 200%), and Spectra Energy (up 40%) have offset losses from the aforementioned stocks. Naturally I wish I had held on to the Home Depot stock that I sold way back in 1986; I had a long term winner and I didn't know it.

The Rest of the Story

As one of the news commentators used to say, "Now for the rest of the story," emphasis has been on the appreciation of stock investments because that is what was fun. More important however, has been overall investments such as land, houses, and reinvestment of dividends and interest from CD's and bonds.

I was very fortunate to have retired in 1984. For a number of years prior to that time my company savings plan had gone nowhere. Then its value increased substantially in the early 80's and at retirement I was able to purchase ten-year municipal bonds at 10¾% return. Inflation subsided in subsequent years and I was then able to make profitable investments in stocks. The stock market continued to rise through the nineties. For the years 2001 and 2002 my losses were modest with reasonable recovery in 2003 and 2004 and significant recovery thereafter.

After reviewing the earlier part of this book I can see that it probably has little purpose except to document the successes and failures of one individual (which hopefully will be of interest and value to at least a select few). Furthermore, because I did not want to reveal my current financial situation for the world to see, there is little indication just how successful were the financial investments. Therefore, after further consideration, additional information is provided herewith. For the record, all gains have been through the IRS.

For the benefit of the reader a comparison of Net Assets in 1977, 1984 at retirement, and 2008 is shown below:

Net Assets

	1977	1984	2008
Personal Items	$ 8,000	$ 10,000	$ 20,000
Real Estate (Excluding House, Lot, and Vacation House)	10,000	2,000	10,000
House Building Lot	8,000	100,000	250,000
House	40,000	100,000	150,000
Vacation House & Lot	0	50,000	300,000
Stocks, Bonds, Savings	20,000	444,000	1,751,000
	$86,000	$706,000	$2,481,000

Asset Growth

Examination of net assets from 1977 until I retired in 1984 reveals a growth of eight-fold ($86,100 to $306,000). Further examination from 1984 until 2008 reveals an additional three-fold growth. Interest, dividends, and stock appreciation certainly account for a part of this growth, but the bulk is due to inflation. The moral is obvious: Find a way to invest something so you can realize the benefits of both growth and inflation.

In 2008 there is a strong temptation to sell half of my remaining Exxon Mobil stock, since I believe it is overpriced. Looking back, however, I see that in 2005 had I not sold 528 shares they would be worth over $14,000 more to me today. Besides, where would I invest the proceeds? The oil stocks have been real winners.

Investment Distribution

To provide insight into my after-retirement financial plan a breakdown of stocks, bonds, savings and other investments is shown below for a number of years.

Financial Investments (in thousands)

	1984	1995	2000	2005	2008
Treasury Notes, Bonds	$ 236	$ 497	$ 516	$ 504	$ 501
CD/Savings	42	8	100	240	395
Cash	18	96	57	17	4
Stocks	123	266	1,009	810	851
Mortgages (Children's Housing)	25	111	16	0	0
	$444	$978	$1,698	$1,571	$1,751

As one can see I took advantage of high interest rates in 1984 but gradually shifted to more stocks in later years. Conservatively though, I continued to maintain a significant bond interest. Wouldn't I have been better off if I had shifted more bond assets to stocks? In retrospect yes, but I slept better knowing that all my eggs were not in one basket. Currently I am looking for security, not growth.

Recent Purchases

Although I am always reluctant to purchase stocks when they are at all-time highs, I recently did just that. For several years I have wanted to invest in solar power and I followed First Solar (FSLR) starting in 2007 at 110. Its price has increased each time I checked and I finally took the plunge at 265 per share. Another stock, Chesapeake Energy (CHK), was recommended in a recent news article and I purchased at 53.5. So far both stocks have done well and I am optimistic about the future.

A recent article (Money Magazine, May 2008) praised New York University economist Nouriel Roubini and commented that he has all his money in a diversified portfolio of index funds. For some time I have considered index funds but never before purchased any. This year when a CD matured I purchased a Fidelity 500 Index Fund and it will be interesting to see how it does. Since the market is way down I believe it may have been good timing.

In Closing

Having grown up during the Depression, I managed money as a matter of necessity. I recall at age 12, selling magazines, I loaned a friend, red-headed "Pecker" a dime. Badgering produced nothing. The last year of high school "Pecker" walked up to me and without saying a word pressed a dime into my hand. I knew immediately that it was settlement of an old debt.

I learned early that anytime I could buy something for a dollar less it would have required me to earn more than $1.50 to be equivalent to that dollar saved. Taxes are everywhere. Anything I could repair would save the entire $1.50. As a kid I vividly recall a statement by a renter in my parent's house. He said he made $200 per month. My comment to myself was, "If I could make that the rest of my life I would be happy." I am happy, although financial security is but a small part of my happiness. I have many friends, a very successful marriage, great kids and grandchildren, and good health. I believe I have invested wisely in every aspect of my life, and the returns have been enormous.

Although I read about the continued growth of stocks I have made an effort to compare my success versus the S&P 500 or with the Dow. I certainly do not compare with some of the real experts. An examination from 1985 to 2008 is rather interesting. To illustrate the following chart depicts my growth (stocks and bonds), which includes the reinvestment of interest and dividends.

<u>Growth Per Year</u>

1985-1988	6.2%
1988-1993	15.5%
1993-1998	9.0%
1998-2003	2.9%
2003-2008	8.1%

In closing, a few words of wisdom:

Inflation is forever.

Try to make it work for you by having something to inflate.

Figure 8—Capital Gains / Losses 2000-2007

Years Held	Stock-Bond Investment	Gain	*Donation Loss
19	General Electric*	5,000	
18	General Electric*	8,300	
18	AXA	5,237	
17	Cappiello-Rushmore Fund		1,367
16	Bell South	6,804	
16	Bell South*	4,900	
16	Exxon Mobil	27,702	
15	Navistar*	3,473	
14	Delta Air Lines Bond		8,123
12	General Electric*	9,700	
12	Ford	3,379	
11	Vodaphone	6,076	
11	Six Stock Funds	126	
10	General Electric*	7,400	
9	ConAgra	2,939	
9	AT&T Wireless		752
8	Johnson & Johnson*	6,450	
7	Regions	1,593	
7	K-Mart		786
7	Oracle	8,016	
7	Cisco		6,998
6	Cisco	2,070	
6	K-Mart		4,244
6	Air Tran	8,105	
6	Intel		6,318
6	Hitachi		289
6	Sun Trust		1,663
4	SBC		3.438
4	Kyphon	4,552	
4	Genentech	12,983	
4	Lucent		10,868
3	Lucent		13,146
3	Stock Fund	298	
3	Disney	2,269	
3	Adobe	3,169	
3	Valero	4,360	
3	Ford		1,400

3	Equity Office Properties		487
2	Lucent		4,746
2	Air Tran		397
2	Miller Industries		2,445
2	EMC Corp.		1,211
2	Sanyo	1,408	
2	Hot Topic	1,430	
2	Freescale	765	
1	Home Depot	3,658	
1	Cerus		191
1	Lucent		10,443

CHAPTER XV

Summary of Financial Gains

1980-1999

	Appreciation
Direct Stock Sales, Net Over	$70,000
Stock to Children	80,000
Stock to Charitable Organizations	40,000
Creekdale House Investment	10,000
Lake House Investment	23,000
Estimated Reinvestment—Funds	20,000
Estimated Dividends (based on 1978 data)	68,000
Big Land Deal	- 39,000 Loss

2000-2007

	Appreciation
Direct Stock Sales, Net	$75,000
Bond Sales	- 8,000 Loss
Dividends	Unknown

APPENDIX 1

Best Estimates of Total Assets—1977

Fair Market Value

	1949	1959	1969	1977
Engagement Ring	$500	$600	$800	$1,000
Wedding Ring	100	100	100	200
Clothes – Family	150	300	500	1,000
Jewelry	50	50	100	500
Automobiles	500	500	2,000	800
Boat, Motor			600	400
Boat, Sail				200
Real Estate			7,000	10,000
Cemetery Lot	100	100	500	1,000
Building Lot		2,000	4,000	8,000
House		15,000	25,000	40,000
Household Furnishings	200	1,500	3,000	3,000
Stocks & Bonds		1,000	6,000	4,000
Life Insurance – Cash Value	1,000	2,000	6,000	1,000
Other Investments				0
Savings	1,000	200	2,000	15,000
Total	$3,600	$22,350	$57,600	$86,100
Mortgage & Car Loan		7,000	1,000	0
Net Assets	$3,600	$15,350	$56,600	$86,100
Salary – Annual	4,000	10,000	19,000	36,000

To compare values with today, one must take inflation into account. To give the reader some appreciation of 1944 salaries and expenses, below is an excerpt from the record of income and expenses just after our marriage.

		Expenses	Income
3/17/44	Train – Atlanta to New York and Return	$37.68	
3/18/44	Hose	1.00	
3/20/44	Lunch and Subway (Subway .05)	.50	
3/30/44	Suit Altered	2.10	
3/30/44	Dinner and Show	2.25	
4/1/44	Dr. Broach	3.00	
4/3/44	Dr. Beasley	5.00	
4/5/44	Socks and Bra	2.00	
4/6/44	Dry Cleaning	2.00	
4/24/44	Shirt	2.00	
4/24/44	Food on Train, Taxi	3.00	
4/26/44	Dry Cleaning	.60	
4/27/44	Bus Fare – Atlanta to Rome, GA	2.50	
4/28/44	Taxi	1.00	
5/1/44	Salary, Month (U.S. Navy Ensign)		175.00
5/17/44	Blouse	3.00	
6/7/44	Watch Crystal	1.00	
6/9/44	Train – Atlanta to New York and Return	39.50	
6/10/44	Shoes	3.00	
6/17/44	Cemetery Lot	120.00	
7/5/44	Train Meals	1.75	
7/7/44	Chiropodist	3.00	
7/8/44	Hotel New Yorker – Double	9.50	
7/9/44	Hotel Edison (NY) – Double	9.00	
7/10/44	Lunch and Subway	.50	
7/18/44	Lunch and Subway	.70	
11/27/44	Hotel, Montreal Canada	5.00	

ABOUT THE AUTHOR

Frank A. Stovall was born in Atlanta, Georgia, where he attended grade schools and college. He served aboard a Navy destroyer escort in World War II and after Navy recall, taught school, worked at Celanese Corporation, Bell South, and Lockheed. While at Lockheed, he was awarded two patents and had published more than a dozen articles on his specialty, Reliability Engineering.

He and his wife, Marjorie, have four children and seven grandchildren. Having grown up during the Depression, he developed a strong work ethic and a healthy respect for integrity, compassion, and money. From the teenage years, he has been active in church work and recently received one of the highest awards for participation in his local church. His favorite sport is tennis and at age 87, still actively competes with those much younger. He holds a BS degree in chemical engineering and an MS in electronics.

www.ingramcontent.com/pod-product-compliance
Lightning Source LLC
Chambersburg PA
CBHW021922170526
45157CB00005B/2142